Pope John Paul II
A Pope for our Time

George Bull

PURNELL

A WORK OF THE OFFICIAL PUBLISHING HOUSE OF THE APOSTOLIC SEE

LIBRERIA EDITRICE VATICANA

The Libreria Editrice Vaticana is the Official Publishing House of the Apostolic See. Its editorial history goes back to 1917 under Canon Law, and was established as an autonomous enterprise in 1926, for the distribution of the publications of the Holy See. These publications include liturgical books (such as missals and breviaries), official acts and documents (such as the *Acta Apostolicae Sedis*, the *Annuario Pontificio*, and the Papal encyclicals) and the teachings of the Supreme Pontiff's personal messages and discourses. Today the Libreria Editrice Vaticana also publishes works ranging from theology, philosophy, biblical studies and spirituality to history, law, literature and art. It was recently commissioned to handle all the author's rights of Karol Wojtyla's works prior to his election as the Supreme Pontiff, John Paul II.

PIETRO MARIETTI PUBLISHING STUDIO

Marietti are one of the oldest Italian publishers. The family firm was founded in 1820 in Turin by Giacinto Marietti and in 1869 his son, Pietro Marietti, was appointed by Pope Pius IX to start the Vatican Polyglot Press with 250 different type-faces ranging from Arabic to Egyptian hieroglyphics, and specialising in the printing of liturgical and religious books. The Pietro Marietti Publishing Studio has now entered the market of international co-publications.

Photographers:
Felici is the only officially authorised photographer of the Holy See.
Mari is the photographer of the daily Vatican newspaper *L'Osservatore Romano*.

Author:
George Bull is a journalist and author of many books including *Inside the Vatican* (Hutchinson).
He is also a director of *The Tablet* and a trustee of *The Universe*.

Designed by:
Anna Caligaris.

Originated by:
Pietro Marietti Publishing Studio
With the collaboration of:
John Hanau

Published by:
Purnell Books, Paulton, Bristol, England BS18 5LQ.

Printed in Italy
by Casa Editrice Marietti, Casale Monferrato

Imprimatur
† Carolus Cavalla, *Episc. Casalensis*

ISBN 0361 05437 8

May God bless Great Britain,
enabling her to fulfil her exalted destiny
in justice and in peace.

Joannes Paulus PP. II

Introduction

Who is the Pope? The term comes from the Latin word for father in the affectionate form papa *as used by a child. In the early days of Christianity it was a term used of the bishops, suggesting that they were regarded as spiritual fathers. From the sixth century, it began to be used only for the Bishop of Rome.*

Roman Catholics believe that the Bishop of Rome, the Pope, because of his position as the successor of St. Peter, exercises by himself alone supreme power over the Church on divine authority. When he teaches on matters of faith or morals he can alone, as well as with his fellow-bishops, invoke the doctrine of infallibility or the divine guarantee that, in certain carefully defined circumstances, he cannot err in his teaching.

The Pope is the spiritual leader of all Roman Catholics and the head of the Holy See, the sovereign body which governs the Catholic Church.

Pope John Paul II has ruled the Catholic Church with a strong hand since his election in 1978, the first non-Italian Pope for centuries. His journeys, which have made him the best known Pope in history, are undertaken chiefly as his personal way of fulfilling the mission of the Holy See in modern times. The mission is to teach and strengthen the Catholic faith.

The Pope's journeys enable him to encourage the practice of the Christian religion, to foster happier relations between different Churches, and to enable people of every kind to see and meet him.

His journeys also help the Pope to discuss the needs and problems of the different national Churches throughout the world, especially as seen by the bishops. They put him in touch with the civil authorities, from heads of government to local officials, with whom he can discuss the attitudes of the Church and seek co-operation in the causes of world peace and development.

This book commemorates the visit of Pope John Paul II to Britain. My knowledge of the Holy See and the Vatican is based on study over many years. This account of the extraordinary life of the Pope and of the great journeys he has made is chiefly based on published information but still reads like a new revelation of one man's absolute dedication to God and total commitment to the service of mankind. My interpretation of the Pope's personality and purposes is meant to stimulate discussion rather than to settle any arguments.

With this Pope, as never before people can see and judge for themselves.

George Bull
London 1982

A Polish boyhood

Poland has given the world great scholars, writers, statesmen, and now, in our times, the first Polish Pope of the Roman Catholic Church, whose personality has elements of all three callings.

Karol Jozef Wojtyla was brought up in the small country town of Wadowice, near the slopes of the Carpathian Mountains and, to the south, the frontier with Czechoslovakia. He was born on 18 May 1920, only two years after the Polish State had regained its independence following a century under foreign domination. The population of Poland, then as now, was largely Roman Catholic. In his family of four, including an older brother, Karol practised and lived the Catholic faith as naturally as breathing.

His father, also called Karol, was a former army lieutenant, a man of strict religious fervour, whose early retirement through ill health meant a life of sacrifice and frugality for himself and his family.

Karol's mother, Emilia, a gentle and quick-witted woman, was a schoolteacher in earlier life. Before Karol's birth, she had lost a newly-born daughter. She called her second son "Lolek", and their closeness had a lasting influence on his development, all the more profound since she died, aged 49, giving birth to a fourth child, a still-born girl. Karol was only nine years old.

Karol's early years were also overshadowed by the death, a few years later, of his brother Edmund who had trained to be a

doctor. Father and son were naturally brought close together through these losses, sharing in their resignation to God's will. But Karol's boyhood was far from subdued or gloomy. It sparkled with promise and achievement from his earliest years.

At elementary and then grammar school (Gymnasium) in Wadowice he studied intently, following the disciplined routine of daily Mass, school and homework. But his studious intelligence was balanced by a spontaneous capacity for friendship and a relish for sport. The young Wojtyla proved himself a good footballer and an enthusiastic skier. Another passion became the theatre, as he zestfully developed his skills as actor, producer and writer. Photographs of him as a boy show the Wojtyla family's good looks in a thoughtful, sensitive face. He developed over these years into a complex strongly motivated personality, his own man, impressing those who know him with his resoluteness and intellect. Among the significant encounters of his boyhood was a meeting during his last term at school with the Archbishop of Cracow, Prince Stefan Sapieha.

In 1938 the family moved to a basement flat in Cracow. The city is one of the most splendid of European centres with magnificent buildings and rich historical associations for both Polish religion and Polish nationalism. Still living frugally with his father, Karol enrolled as a student at the famous Jagiellonian University, named after the mediaeval Grand Duke who married Poland's saintly Queen Jadwiga. The brilliance of its university had made Cracow the pre-eminent cultural centre of Poland.

Karol decided to study Polish language and literature, with philosophy as an additional subject.

He easily made a fresh circle of friends and continued his interest in poetry, the theatre and sport. And then, in 1939, his life like the lives of millions in Europe was abruptly and brutally reshaped when the invasion of Poland by Nazi Germany began the Second World War.

1 The parish church in the town of Wadowice in Poland, where Karol Wojtyla was born.

2 With his mother who died when Karol was only 9 years old.

3 Karol dressed for his first communion.

4 As a young man, out walking with his aunt.

Worker and priest

The Russian and Germans divided Poland between them, in the fourth and most callous partition of Poland's history. The Jagiellonian University, physically and symbolically the centre of Poland's independent culture, would obviously suffer at the invaders' hands. In the winter of 1939 the German Gestapo rounded up and arrested its academic staff of about 180 professors and other teachers of whom about a tenth died in concentration camps before their release after months of suffering. The university, with the help of the survivors, went underground with clandestine classes and examinations, defying Nazi occupiers sworn to exterminate the Polish ruling classes, the clergy and the nobles, the intellectuals and the Jews.

As a student, Karol Wojtyla risked the same kind of fate as the university teachers, imprisonment, deportation, or death. Like thousands of others, he sought work as a labourer, securing a vital work-card and finding a job in a limestone quarry outside Cracow, belonging to the Solway company. His first work in the cold winter of 1940 was hewing and carting rock; later he was made an assistant to the shot firer; and then in 1942 he was transferred to the company's water-

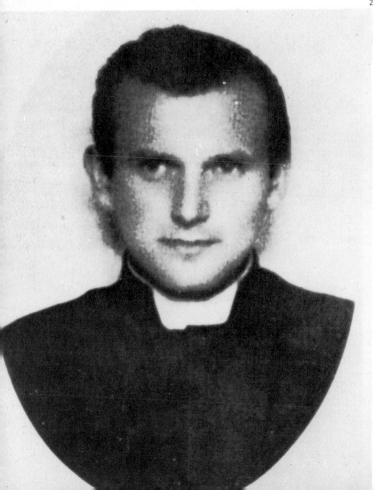

purification department where he continued in physical work, carrying buckets of lime and mixing chemicals.

In a poem called *The Quarry*, Karol used his experience of grinding physical work and violent contact with stone to exult in human energy and intellect and in the arduous triumph of love and the dignity of the worker.

This was the period of the young adult Wojtyla's protracted physical and mental toughening in adversity. During the war years, he once came near to death when, going home exhausted after work, he was hit by a tram and his skull fractured; in another accident he was again seriously injured.

He continued all the while to write poetry, to enjoy the activities of a secret, resistance, theatre group, and to study assiduously. Several warm personal friendships influenced his life, including his bond with the active Catholic organiser, Jan Tyranowski, who especially urged his companions to read the writings of St John of

1 As an alter boy at the age of 11.

2 In 1945, as a young man at the seminary.

3 In 1946, while still at the seminary, Karol became a deacon.

4 At 38 years old, Karol Wojtyla was made Bishop of Cracow.

the Cross. This Spanish mystic and poet held an enduring appeal for Karol, whose thoughts began to move towards the idea of becoming a priest.

In the summer of 1944, after the Warsaw rising against the Germans, Karol, with several other young Poles, was protected against an intensified campaign of deportation by Archbishop Sapieha who provided refuge in his episcopal palace.

Soon after, the war ended with the defeat of the Axis powers and Russian troops swept across a Poland which had seen over six million of its people, including three million Jews, killed by the Germans.

Karol Wojtyla's decision to become a priest had been taken while he was still working for the chemical company. His father had

1   At prayer in his church at Wadowice. Karol Wojtyla was the youngest bishop in Poland at this time.

2   The great love of children which John Paul II has always shown was apparent even in the early days of his career.

3   Karol Wojtyla was made a cardinal by Pope Paul VI in 1967.

died from a stroke in 1941 and the shock and sorrow of this loss — he spent a night kneeling in prayer — prompted his enrolment in an underground seminary.

By 1946, Karol had completed his studies in the Theology Department of the re-opened University of Cracow. He passed his examinations in August 1946 — with very distinguished results — and was ordained priest at the age of 26 by Archbishop Sapieha (soon after to be made a cardinal) on 1 November, All Saints' Day. The following Sunday he said Mass at the parish Church of Wadowice.

From all over the world exceptionally promising priests are sent by their bishops to study in Rome, near the Vatican City State and the headquarters of the Holy See. Father Wojtyla's capacity for leadership and hard work and his questing intelligence convinced Cardinal Sapieha that he was an ideal candidate for the Pontifical University of St Thomas Aquinas, known as the Angelicum. In the charge of the Dominican friars, this university, with his library of over 130,000 volumes, was called by a former Pope ''the home of St Thomas'', the greatest theologian and philosopher of the Catholic Church. It has three faculties, philosophy, theology and Canon Law, the law of the Church.

In Rome, studying at the Angelicum and living at the Belgian College on Via G.B. Pagano, Father Wojtyla came under the forceful intellectual influence of the Angelicum's director of studies, the French Dominican Garrigou-Lagrange, a formidable exponent of the Thomist thinking and defender of Catholic dogmatic teaching. The ruling Pontiff was Eugenio Pacelli, Pius XII, and the Roman atmosphere was one of traditional piety and unquestioning loyalty centred on the person of the Pope.

Walking briskly to and fro between the Angelicum and the Belgian College every day, Father Wojtyla worked studiously on his doctoral thesis concerning the teaching about faith in the writings of St John of the Cross. He came to know Rome and the Italian language quite well, to learn and perfect his French, and to gather a wide, international circle of acquaintances and friends, including the Belgian priest, Father Marcel Uylenbroeck, who was chaplain general of the worldwide

Christian Workers organisation. He spent some time in France, partly on holiday, partly to help some stranded Polish refugees, a group of miners.

In Rome, Father Wojtyla's chief intellectual development came through his deepening understanding of the theology of St Thomas Aquinas. Three decades later, after he had become Pope John Paul II, he was to affirm his commitment to the "perennial philosophy" of Aquinas before a group of cardinals called to the Angelicum to celebrate the hundredth anniversary of the publication of Pope Leo XIII's encyclical *Aeterni Patris*.

In Poland, while Father Wojtyla was away in Rome, a Commu-

nist "People's Republic" had been imposed and tensions were rising between the Church and the government as publications were censored, religious education was crushed, Church property seized and many priests imprisoned. There was also some strain between Church leaders in Poland and the Vatican authorities over the ecclesiastical policy that should be adopted towards the former German territories now absorbed by Poland. But Father Wojtyla's first post on his return to Poland in 1948 was as curate in the small village of Niegiwic, 120 miles from Cracow. There are charming stories from this time of the young priest's poverty and unworldliness, as he accepted pre-

sents only to give them away again, passed on the fruits of his erudition in the pulpit, took his turn working in the fields to help out, and suggested that his parishioners should and could build a new church to celebrate their parish priest's Golden Jubilee.

Father Wojtyla's rise in the hierarchy of the Catholic Church was soon to begin, however. The thesis he had finished in Rome earned him a doctorate from the theological department of the University of Cracow, and he was called back to Cracow by Cardinal Sapieha to serve in the parish of St Florian's. There, with exceptional kindliness and drive, he did what thousands of Catholic curates do throughout the world,

14

year in and year out: assist the parish priest, say Mass and administer the sacraments, organise functions for the young and the old, and listen to the hopes and anxieties of people needing to be comforted or encouraged. Father Wojtyla's eloquent, carefully structured preaching, with his stress on the power and love of God and the need for renunciation, began to make his name known throughout the diocese.

Cardinal Sapieha, who had fought doggedly and proudly for his Christian principles against first the German dictatorship and then the imposition of Communism, died in 1951. Soon after, Father Wojtyla was transferred to the parish of St Catherine's in another part of Cracow and requested to take up the regular study of philosophy again, and to work towards another degree. For the next six years he lived with his former professor, Father Rozycki.

He sustained his interest in writing poetry and plays, and in outdoor sports whenever he could. More and more, he focused on philosophy, on exploring the works of the Christian existentialist and personalist thinkers. He was notably stimulated by a German Catholic thinker called Max Scheler who had a stormy relationship with the Church though he enriched the thinking of many Catholic philosophers on the nature of the spiritual tensions in man and his creative relationship with God.

During these years, Father Wojtyla lived the life of a sportive young university don, teaching social ethics at the seminary in Cracow, and also hurrying off a considerable distance to lecture at the Catholic University of Lublin. His chase after philosophical understanding, linking contemporary explorations with Thomist thought, was deeply serious and painstaking. But his academic duties kept him agreeably in touch with the young, especially with the students whose responses to him were always admiring and affectionate.

Father Wojtyla was enjoying a canoeing holiday on the Masurian lakes with some students when he was called to see the Primate of Poland, Cardinal Stefan Wyszynski, to learn about his appointment to the post of Auxiliary Bishop of Cracow. He was consecrated as auxiliary to Archbishop Baziak in Wawel Cathedral on 28 September 1958. On his coat of arms, he used the letter M and the Latin words, *Totus tuus* (all for you), to signify his devotion to the Virgin Mary, or to Our Lady as Catholics say. With genuine reluctance, he accepted that he must move from his modest flat to the episcopal palace, but he took his skis with him.

1   *With Pope John Paul I.*

2   *Following the death of Pope John Paul I, Cardinal Wojtyla is seen here on the way to the Sistine Chapel where the cardinals will meet to elect a new pope.*

The election of a Polish Pope

1 The new Pope, John Paul II,
appears on the balcony of St Peter's
for the first time.

2 A solemn moment at a
concelebration in St Peter's Square.

Karol Wojtyla threw himself into
the work of a bishop with all the
keen-eyed vigour he brought to
sport. His position gave him con-
stant excuses for meeting, getting
to know and influencing a range
of people of all classes and profes-
sions. He grabbed the opportuni-
ties gladly. His weekly parties,
with their symbolic religious sharing of wine and wafers of unlea-
vened bread, became famous. In
1960, he published his first book
on *Love and Responsibility*, so
maintaining his stake in the world
of study and literature just as he
still fostered his links with students and intellectuals while per-
forming the demanding pastoral
duties of a conscientious, out-
going bishop.

As a bishop, Wojtyla was summoned, with about three thousand of his fellow-bishops, to the
meeting of the Second Vatican
Council in St Peter's Basilica in
Rome in October 1962. The
Council, whose sessions lasted
from 1962 to 1965, was summoned by Pope John XXIII and con-
cluded by his successor Pope Paul
VI. The debates and declarations
of the Second Vatican Council
were aimed at helping the *aggior-
namento* or renewal of the Catholic Church prayed for by Pope
John XXIII. They fostered fresh
thinking and initiatives throughout the Church on momentous issues ranging from relations with
other Christians and believers,
with non-believers even, to Christian responsibilities in regard to
world poverty and peace. The teaching of the bishops is preserved
in 16 documents of immense ove-

1 *In front of St Peter's.*

2 *Inside St Peter's.*

rall theological richness and importance.

Bishop Wojtyla took part enthusiastically in the work of the Council and has many times since pledged himself, as bishop and Pope, to the continuance of its dynamic purposes.

On the eve of the Second Vatican Council, Bishop Wojtyla was made Acting Archbishop of Cracow, following the death of Archbishop Baziak. He made his chief contributions to the Council's work in the second session in 1963 when he especially contributed to the debates on the key Council document concerning the nature of the Church, called *Lumen Gentium*, and those on religious liberty. Later, he wrote a book on the Council entitled *Sources of*

Renewal which carefully reported the debates and urged the implementation of the Council's wishes.

In January 1964 Karol Wojtyla was made Archbishop of Cracow. He was respectfully intimate with Cardinal Wyszynski who had borne the brunt of Communist oppression, including imprisonment, and who tended to be more conservative than Wojtyla in his attitude to liturgical changes, including offering the Mass in Polish instead of Latin. After he became Archbishop, Wojtyla increasingly shared with the Cardinal the burden of national leadership of the Catholic Church — constantly at odds with the Communist authorities — while moving in his own way to carry out the practical initiatives suggested by the Vatican Council. He encouraged more activity by the laity in the affairs of the Church, especially through regular conferences to investigate in common their own professional concerns.

On 29 May 1967 the news came from Rome that Karol Wojtyla was one of the 27 new cardinals created by Pope Paul VI. This meant that he had been called by the Pope to act as one of his assistants in the administration of the Catholic Church, and that as a member of the Sacred College he would be summoned to take part in the future election of a Pope. Cardinals are regarded as the princes of the Catholic Church, distinguished to the eye by their cassocks of scarlet or purple. From among the cardinals the Pope must be chosen, the Supreme Pontiff of the Church.

Cardinal Wojtyla proved an exemplary Archbishop of his diocese of Cracow. He dealt cautiously with the pressures on the Church as the Polish Communist leadership changed from Wladislaw Gomulka to Edward Gierek after the workers' violent riots of 1970. He endeavoured to improve the Church's own communications with the faithful by holding a Synod, or consultative council, in his own Archdiocese. The exercise was carefully planned; study groups and parish committees sprang up; and the reality grew of more extensive understanding and collaboration between the priests and the laity than ever in the past.

In the series of Synods held in Rome for the bishops to advise the Pope and discuss the affairs of the Church in a collegial atmosphere, Cardinal Wojtyla played a lively role as the elected representative of the Polish hierarchy. In 1971, he was elected to the secretariat of the Bishops' Synod in Rome. He began travelling extensively outside Poland and Europe, to Australia, New Guinea and the Philippines, for example, in 1973; to Harvard in the United States to give a lecture at a summer school. In 1976 he travelled to Philadelphia for a Eucharistic Congress. The same year he was invited by Pope Paul VI to give the Lenten "retreat" sermons to the Roman Curia (the Vatican's top civil servants) and his Holiness himself. These were published under the title *A Sign of Contradiction*.

The Cardinal developed into a flexible and sensitive but strict pastor of his flock, a budding world traveller, an emphatically orthodox thinker and writer, with wide artistic sympathies, and an impressive orator increasingly to the fore in the minds of the prelates of the Catholic Church. He also seemed always to be glowing with health.

In 1976 Cardinal Wojtyla consecrated a beautiful new church in the Polish steel town of Nowa Huta, a decade after the authorities had given their permission for this mark of the Church's strength among the workers and the staunchness of the workers' Catholic belief.

2

On 6 August 1978, Pope Paul VI died and Cardinal Wojtyla left for the Conclave in Rome, looking tired, it was said, and apprehensive about what might be in store. The cardinals chose as the new Pontiff a courteous, smiling Italian from the north, the self-effacing Patriarch of Venice, Albino Luciani. But sadly John Paul I died after reigning for only 33 days. It seemed that he was overwhelmed by the daunting responsibilities of his office.

During these weeks, on 28 September 1978 Cardinal Wojtyla celebrated his 20th anniversary as a bishop. On 16 October after two days of waiting, the crowd in St Peter's Square in Rome saw white smoke swirling from the chimney of the Sistine Chapel and knew that a new Pope had been elected. This had happened after eight ballots and on the second day of the Conclave. (Popes are normally elected by the cardinals locked up in the Sistine Chapel, by the system of "scrutiny", i.e. two votes being taken each morning and two each afternoon until one candidate receives a majority of two-thirds plus one vote.)

After the cardinals made their decision, Cardinal Wojtyla slowly left the Sistine Chapel, dressed in the same way as the other cardinals, to return a few moments later wearing the simple white cassock of Pope. In the evening, at the end of the second day of voting, St Peter's Square was bathed in moonlight. The new Pope was announced to the city and the world — *Urbi et Orbi* — in the customary manner, by the dean of the Sacred College, Cardinal Pericle Felici. Waiting quietly to greet the crowd in St Peter's, the newly elected Polish Pope heard the soft-voiced Italian cardinal announce in Latin "a great joy" ("*Nuntio vobis gaudium magnum. Habemus Papam*") "we have a Pope..." Then Karol Wojtyla found himself standing on the balcony at the front of St Peter's, giving his blessing to the

people, talking to them in Italian instead of the traditional Latin, and confiding that he had been ready to become the new Pope, taking the name John Paul II, ''in the spirit of obedience to the Lord and total faithfulness to Mary our most holy Mother.''

The election of the first Polish Pope and the first non-Italian Pope for over four centuries bemused, delighted and stunned people all over the world. Within the Vatican, the first of the cardinals to pay personal homage to him when he was installed as Pope on Sunday 22 October, was Cardinal Wyszynski, whom John Paul II lifted to his feet and kissed on the hand in a typical act of spontaneous compassion, love and respect.

1   The Pope at his first Mass in the Sistine Chapel, attended by the cardinals.

2   From the balcony of St Peter's.

3 . On the day following the election Cardinal Wyszinski pays homage to the new Pope.

The Holy See and City State

For a while, before the settlement in 1929 between the Italian State and the Papacy of claims of territory and jurisdiction, the popes were called the prisoners of the Vatican. This is clearly not so today and least of all in the case of Pope John Paul II who travels so constantly throughout the world. Nonetheless the cardinal who wakes up in the Vatican Palace, awa-re that he has just been elected Pope, knows that he will never return for good to his own people: he belongs to the Church and the world, and he will be buried under St Peter's when he dies, near to the tomb believed to be the tomb of the Chief of the Apostles, St Peter himself.

The Vatican is the Pope's home and is also the headquarters of the

1 *Mass in St Peter's.*

2 *With the faithful in St Peter's Square.*

administration of the universal Catholic Church. The Pope is elected to be Bishop of Rome and, as such, the successor to St Peter is the supreme pastor of the Catholic Church. As well as being head of the Holy See the Pope is sovereign head of the little Vatican City State, whose 108 acres of land provide the Papacy with a symbol of independence and a base for its artistic heritage and its necessary physical administration.

The Vatican City State, rising gently along the hillside from the historically variegated area of Rome west of the Tiber, is a marvellous complex of gardens and piazzas, Renaissance and Baroque fountains and ancient walls, mu-seums and monuments, chapels and palaces, spread around the great Church of St Peter's and protected by security police and the famous Swiss Guards. Many of the Curial cardinals who help the Pope to govern the Church live there, and it contains numerous offices for important departments of the government of the Church as well as blocks of shops, barracks, and plant for printing and electricity. The Vatican has its own railway station and heliport.

The Vatican, nonetheless, is above all a power-house of prayer based on the year-round activities of the Pope himself, whose offices and private rooms are in the Apo-

1 The Pope during the Via Crucis.

2-3 The Pope with a group of his own personal bodyguards, the Swiss Guards, who number 100 strong.

stolic Palace looking over the great square of St Peter's.

From here, where his life is centred on prayer and preaching, the Pope governs the whole of the Catholic Church through the bishops in different countries and through the administrators of the Holy See, the cardinals and officials of the Roman Curia.

It is hard to describe a "typical" day in the life of a Pope, especially in the case of John Paul II who is so spontaneous, creative and adventurous. When

the Pope is in the Vatican, however, he begins each day early in the morning with an hour or more of solitary prayer. A few of his close attendants then join him for Mass in the austere, bright, private chapel. Closest to the Pope, in his day-to-day life, are two private secretaries (who are priests), a group of Polish nuns of the Maria Bambina order, the prelate who is the head of the Pontifical Household and, on vital official business, the Cardinal Secretary of State whose duties are rather like

those of a Prime Minister and Foreign Affairs Minister.

Pope John Paul II has tended to vary the routine as much as possible. He has a habit of unexpectedly inviting guests to join him for breakfast or dinner. Soon after he became Pope, he had a swimming pool built at the Papal summer residence and retreat, the beautiful villa of Castel Gandolfo, which houses the famous Vatican Observatory. He uses the Vatican gardens for brisk exercise.

After a good breakfast, the Pope

reads the many documents and letters brought to his attention in a flow of communications from all over the world. In a courteous and inquiring manner, he then starts his "audiences" of the day, before a midday meal which is invariably an opportunity for invited people to meet the Pope and talk informally.

The audiences are an essential and varied part of the fabric of the Pope's life. They range from his daily meetings with the chief Vatican officials to the regular discussions with the cardinals and *monsignori* of the Curia, both individually and collectively, to meetings with all the Catholic bishops of the world coming regularly to see the Supreme Pontiff from their different continents and nations.

As head of the Holy See and ruler of the Vatican City State, the Pope has his diplomatic and religious representatives posted to hundreds of countries and to scores of institutions and in turn receives representatives from all parts of the world. Much of his time is spent in discussions and negotiations about the position of the Catholic Church or international problems concerning which the advice or mediation of the Church may be sought.

But the audiences of the Pope are not just for the bishops and the diplomats. Basic to the Holy Father's work are the gatherings of the Catholic faithful, of devout pilgrims, or curious tourists, flocking to the Basilica of St Peter's and the Vatican to hear the words of Pope John Paul II.

Thousands of people seek and are granted an audience with the Pope privately or in special groups every week. Best known to the world and most spectacular are

2

3

1   With Queen Elizabeth and
Prince Philip on their visit to Rome
in 1980.

2   The Pope demonstrates his
fondness for children.

3   With Mother Teresa of
Calcutta.

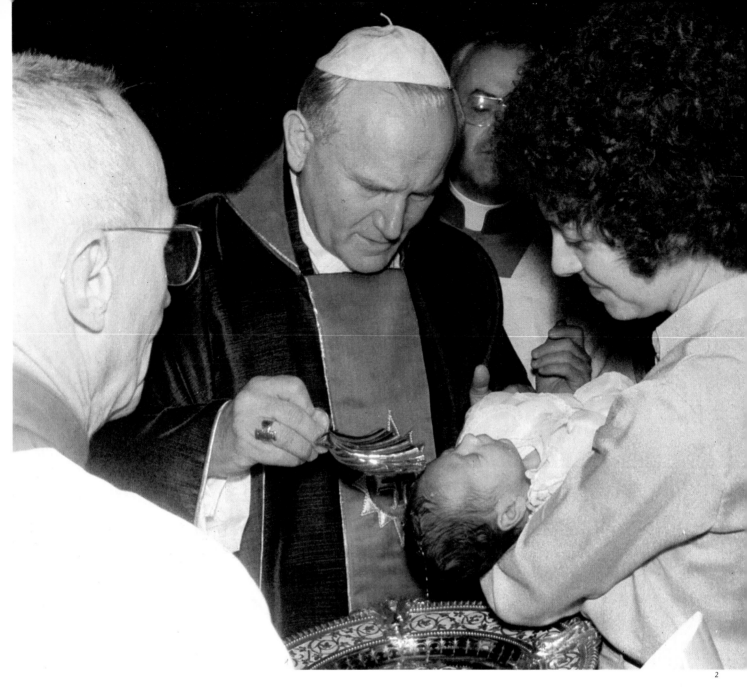

the general audiences given to vast crowds every Wednesday, both in the huge modern audience hall and in the great square of St Peter's. On these occasions the Pope moves around and greets people informally and then delivers an address (later published) dealing with spiritual and theological issues.

Each Sunday at noon the Pope leads the people in prayer, saying the *Angelus*, the prayer of the Virgin Mary, from the balcony of his apartment. Sometimes he will himself hear people's confessions in one of the confessional "boxes" of St Peter's.

These lines of communication, in prayer and sermon, form vital parts of the Pope's ceaseless contact with the faithful of the Catholic Church and the whole of the world — from quiet talks to the drafting and promulgating of the "encyclicals" which are the richest source for establishing the authoritative beliefs of the Catholic Church.

In sum, the Pope's generous but joyfully performed duties within the Vatican are ceremonial, pastoral, administrative and diplomatic. To these, more than any Pope in the past, Pope John Paul II has added what he sees as the urgent duty of a Pope to travel the world, primarily to preach the word of Christ and to reinforce His teaching.

1-2 As often as possible Pope John Paul officiates at ceremonies for ordinary people. Here he conducts a baptism and a Holy Communion. This is one of the Pope's ways of showing his great love and concern for all people everywhere.

A pilgrim around the world

The journeys of Pope John Paul II spring from the international responsibilities of the modern Papacy. Throughout history, the Holy See has exerted its authority over the local communities of the Catholic Church in many lands. It has also used its religions and moral autority to help governments and international organisations along the ways of peace. In the history of Europe, the Papacy has played a creative role since the Middle Ages and the Renaissance in the processes and development of diplomacy.

Today the Vatican is in the middle of a worldwide diplomatic network and directly or indirectly involved in issues of great human concern which range from disarmament proposals to agricultural and population policies.

There are over 100 ''missions'' of the Holy See posted throughout the world, called either apostolic delegations (with solely ecclesiastical duties) or nunciatures (with diplomatic functions as well).

The voice of the Holy See is also heard through the scores of observers or representatives which the Vatican sends to world conferences, such as that on the Law of the Sea, and to permanent organisations including the International Postal Union.

Contacts and understanding between the Holy See and different countries of the world are developed by nearly 100 diplomatic representatives attached in one form or another by their governments to the Vatican.

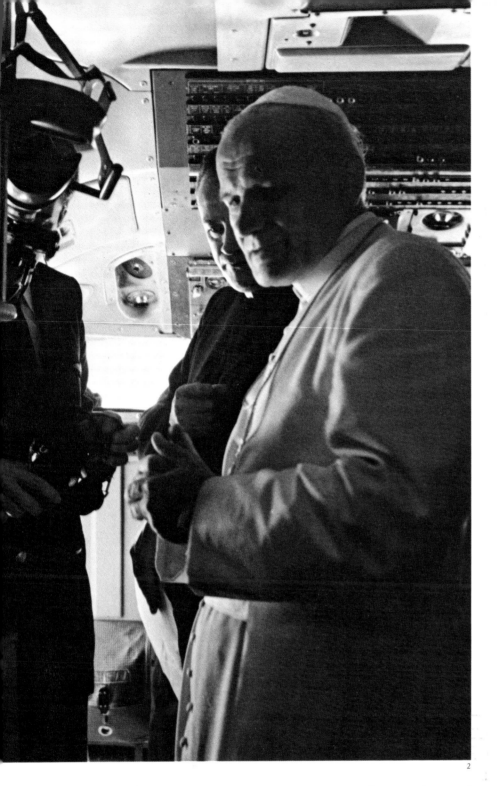

ral: directed, in other words, to the spiritual care of his Christian "flock" in all parts of the world.

The task which the Pope is fulfilling as he travels in person to see as many as possible of the members of the Catholic faith is to encourage and exemplify the fundamental unity of the Church, to foster Christian practice and morality, and to express the spirit of ecumenism, the understanding and tolerance which reach out to other faiths.

From the start of his pontificate, Pope John Paul II made it plain that he would emulate Pope Paul VI who had travelled to America, the Holy Land and India during his historic pontificate which began with the challenging decisions of the Second Vatican Council. As Bishop of Rome, he was resolved to keep closely in touch with his own parishes and people. But soon the Church and the world were to grow accustomed to the frequent departures of the Pope from the Vatican City State, watched on his way and at his destination by the eyes of millions.

Rarely, when the Pope is visiting a country, does he fail to signal that he sees himself as a pilgrim, pressing on through time and space, to an invisible goal. He visits and prays at the famous shrines and pilgrimage centres: Czestochowa in Poland, Knock in Ireland, Lourdes in France, Fatima in Portugal.

Kissing the soil in country after country, praying at the national shrines, always close to the people who have come to see him, the Pope expresses deeply traditional values relating to patriotism, family piety, priesthood and the nature of the Papacy itself, in his own open and transforming manner.

His acts always seem spontaneous, but he adapts to what he sees as the old values of all the Christian communities he visits, the carefully prepared message that he brings.

1-2 While travelling the Pope takes time to relax and prepare for his next stop, but he still finds time to take an interest in what is going on.

The journeys of Pope John Paul II have added a fresh dimension to this complex involvement of the Holy See in international affairs.

His travels help the Pope to examine freshly and at first hand the situation and needs of the local churches. They enable him to discuss the Church's policies and teaching with the civil authorities.

The Pope's motives and purposes in travelling from Rome so often and so far are primarily pasto-

In January 1979, only three months after his election, John Paul II set out on his first overseas visit as Pope to Mexico, a country of 60 million, mostly Catholic, inhabitants, with violent contrasts of climate and geography, and a history of splendour and savagery, close woven with that of the Catholic Church.

The immediate reason for the visit to Mexico was the Pope's desire to make a "pilgrimage of faith", to an important conference of bishops at Puebla, Mexico's oldest diocese.

Of all the world's Roman Catholics, about half live in Central and South America, where exist some of the most unjust disparities of wealth and extremes of political oppression in the world.

Hence the importance of this visit to the Holy See which had seen the Latin American bishops at an earlier conference (held at Medellin, Columbia in 1968) call insistently for social and political reform. In the debate about religion and reform, the arguments grew as to how far Catholic bishops and priests should support or undertake political activities for the ends of justice, even with the danger of encouraging violence. There were arguments for and against the Church's acceptance of a new, socially committed and politically engaged "theology of liberation".

From Rome, the Pope flew first to the Dominican Republic, which has close associations with the early Christian history of the

New World, and then on to Mexico where he arrived on 25 January. This was declared a day of national rejoicing by the Government.

The Pope was formally greeted by the President of Mexico; received by his fellow-bishops; and driven south from Mexico City the next day through enthusiastic crowds numbering millions of people. His first goal was the image and sanctuary of the Virgin at Guadalupe.

The beautiful tradition of Guadalupe is that of an old Indian in the sixteenth century seeing, on a hilltop near Mexico City, a vision of the Virgin Mary who told him he should have the bishop build a church on the spot, and then, when she appeared again, that he

1

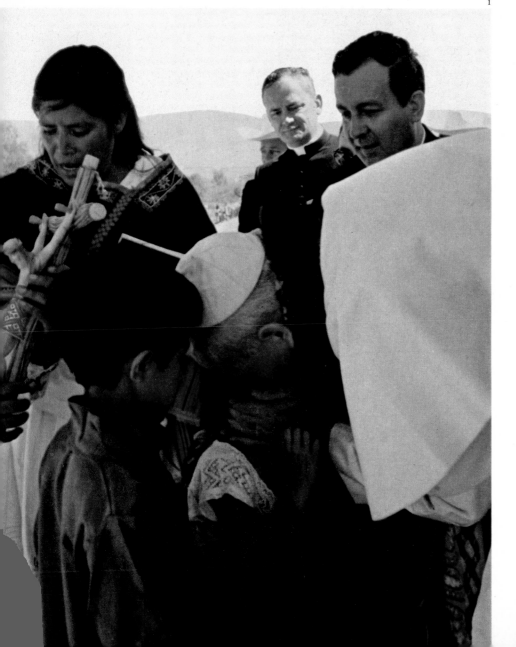

1   The Pope kisses an Indian child in Mexico.

2   Pope John Paul was presented with an Indian headdress in Oaxaca.

3   At Guilapan 300.000 Indians gathered to meet Pope John Paul. The Pope spoke of his great concern for the poverty and hard conditions of the poor people of Mexico.

2

3

should pick flowers and take them to the bishop. Having obeyed, he shook the roses from his apron, and the image of the Virgin was revealed upon it.

At Guadalupe, and later during his Mexican journey when he met the Indians of Guilapan, Pope John Paul II spoke directly to people of simple faith to rehearse the strongly rooted traditional Catholic practices and dogmatic beliefs that he shares with them.

When he became the Supreme Pontiff Romans started to call him "the festive Pope", and his time in Mexico was also partly a carnival for the people as well as a pilgrimage for him.

The other main aspect of the pilgrimage was the Pope's message when he opened the Latin American bishops' conference on 28 January. In his statements he balanced his demands for loyalty and unity within the Church, and

the eschewal of violence and overt political activities by the priests, with a heartfelt insistence on the inherent dignity of man and on human rights. Human improvement must come through respect for the teaching of the Church and through love for others.

Having drawn the lines in this way, the Pope put great emphasis in later speeches on the concern of the Church for the poor and its capacity to achieve reform through

1

its recent teachings and traditional unity. By Mexican Indians — half a million came to see him in Oaxaca — he was greeted with the words: "You are the voice of those who are silent". He told them of their right to land and their right to demand the reforms that would secure a better society. He attacked the "powerful classes which sometimes hold lands unproductive, keeping back the bread that so many families lack…".

To office and industrial workers of Monterrey, in the north of Mexico, near the frontier with the United States, Pope John Paul again extolled the dignity of labour. He compared Monterrey with Nova Huta in his native Poland; defended the workers' freedom to organise; offered the aid of the Church to the working-class movement; and assured them of the love of God, of Christ, and of the Virgin Mary.

1　In the cathedral at Guadalajara Pope John Paul greets some nuns from an enclosed order.

2　In Guadalajara the Pope is welcomed to the Jalisco football stadium by thousands of workers and their families.

From addressing crowds in the dried-up river bed of the Rio Santa Caterina at Monterrey, a few months later, on 2 June 1979, the Pope was being welcomed by his own countrymen in Poland. John Paul II had left little doubt that he would return to Poland. The occasion was the 900th anniversary of the martyrdom of St Stanislaus, Bishop of Cracow, patron saint of the Poles.

The nine days that the Pope spent in Poland were in some ways a triumphant progress, as the Poles displayed a natural pride in Karol Wojtyla's presence among them. Again, for the Pope himself, it was an opportunity to proclaim the linkage between the liberation of man and the practice of religion. It was also a testing of the relationship between Church and State in Poland. It seems certain that the visit encouraged the Poles in their resistance to political constraint and corruption in the following strife-torn years.

For Poland, the lines of communication to the non-Communist world had been vitally strengthened by the Papal election of 1979, but above all it had stiffened the Poles' own pride and resolve. The affection shown to the Pope throughout Poland seemed unbounded.

On arrival, after the official welcome by the Polish President, he celebrated Mass in Victory Square in Warsaw, a great rallying-point and ceremonial centre, dignified by its tomb of the Unknown Soldier. The response of the crowd of about 200 thousand people was ecstatic as he preached to them and through them about the meaninglessness of history without Christ.

At Gniezno, the ancient capital of Poland, St Adalbert of Bohemia first brought Christianity to the Polish Slavs. Appropriately, John Paul II spoke here at the cathedral, celebrating an open-air Mass for the young and stressing

his hopes for the end of divisions between Christians of East and West. It was a day of prayer and singing, of deep emotion stirred by Polish patriotism and religious fervour at the time of Pentecost.

The Pope said of himself: "Pope John Paul II, a Slav, a son of the Polish nation, feels how deeply fixed in the ground of history are the roots of his origin, how many centuries stand behind the word of the Holy Spirit proclaimed by him from St Peter's Vatican Hill and here at Gniezno, from the hill of Lech...".

On 4 June the Pope presided at a concelebrated Mass at the Marian shrine of Jasna Góra in Czestochowa. Jasna Góra — the hill of light — is the sanctuary of the Black Madonna, an icon brought from the Ukraine in the fourteenth century by a prince who built a chapel and founded a monastery for its care. The Black Madonna, probably dating from the ninth century, was traditionally

1 *A huge crowd gathers for Mass at Blania Krakowstie.*

2 *A moment of peace.*

Pope John Paul celebrates Mass
at the ninth centenary of St
Stanislaus at Wawel.

said to have been painted by St Luke. In the seventeenth century, Our Lady of Czestochowa was proclaimed Queen of Poland. Since then, she has been for Catholics the symbol of Polish nationalism and religious freedom, and the icon has been constantly venerated.

In his homily after the Gospel, the Pope talked of the "special presence" of the Virgin Mary at Czestochowa in the mystery of Christ and the Church. He particularly linked to the shrine the names of recent Popes, as if strengthening the spiritual supports for Poland from Rome. He said that one heard the heart of the Polish nation beating in the heart of the Mother; and talked of the Catholic Church as "our spiritual Mother in the likeness of the Mother of the Eternal Word".

After a joyful visit to Cracow and to his own native town and first diocese of Wadowice, exuberantly welcomed and fêted in both, the Pope moved physically and emotionally to a starkly different plane of past and present: to Auschwitz, which he called the "Golgotha of the modern world."

Here the Pope knelt and prayed by the spot where thousands had been shot, including the priest Maximilian Kolbe who had given his life in 1941 for another prisoner. The Pope concelebrated Mass near to where the Nazi death trains had arrived, with scores of priests who had survived their ordeal in the camp. Thousands of Poles wearing the striped prison clothes of the inmates of Auschwitz were among the million who witnessed the Pope say Mass. In his homily he talked of Father Kolbe's victory at Oswiecim (Auschwitz) won through faith and love, as had been the victories of other victims.

Auschwitz, Pope John Paul II reminded his silent, brooding congregation, was in the diocese he himself had left to go to the See of St Peter. It was no wonder

39

1   The Pope prays by the memorial tablets to the dead of the former concentration camp at Dachau.

2   Pope John Paul leaves flowers outside the cell of Maximilian Kolbe, the martyred Polish priest.

3   Gifts of flowers from Polish children.

1

2

that the first words of his first encyclical should be *Redemptor Hominis* (The Redeemer of Mankind) and that he should have dedicated it ''to the cause of man, to the dignity of man...''.

From Poland's students to the peasant farmers, from the factory workers to the Polish bishops in conference, up and down the country, the Pope encountered his fellow Poles in their millions and left an impression of warmth and accessibility.

His last address, in Cracow, on Sunday 10 June, was given to a crowd of about three million, in the park in the city's centre. He gave a philosophical discourse on the nature of the human person as a free and rational being with a destiny and goal. He said that a person's knowledge and choices were bound up with the living traditions of his or her own country. He cited Poland's great saints Stanislaus and Adalbert as witnesses of Christ. Poland had been baptised a thousand years before; Poland had been confirmed. He appealed to all Poles to accept the ''spiritual legacy'' which was their own country.

On 10 June, welcomed among others by the Italian Prime Minister, the Pope arrived at Ciampino Airport. As always, his round of official tasks within the Vatican imposed itself at once. On Sunday 13 June he was once more holding a general audience in St Peter's Square, walking towards the crowds and reminding his hearers that it was in Poland that he had learned his love of the Eucharist. He met and touched scores of pilgrims.

The Pope's fellow-Poles would soon be pressing him to return to Poland. Meanwhile the Pope had already been urged by Cardinal O'Fiaich, Archbishop of Armagh, to accept the Irish bishops' invitation to come to Ireland. The cardinal talked warmly to the Pope of the shrine of Knock. When the news of his forthcoming visit to Ireland was announced, thoughts turned everywhere to what the Pope would say and how he could influence the violence in the North of Ireland, battening on religious differences between Catholic and Protestant.

The Pope arrived at Dublin on 29 September, the day after the first anniversary of the death of Pope John Paul I. His first words were in praise of the "glorious contribution" made by Ireland over the centuries to the sprea-

ding of the Catholic faith. In Dublin, he talked to religious and political leaders and spent some hours with Polish emigrants and handicapped children. In Phoenix Park, before over a million people, he put the greatest stress on the dangers of materialism. Meeting thousands of young people in Galway, on the west coast of Ireland, he affirmed the strength of his belief in youth and warned them against the abuse of drugs, alcohol and sex.

At the shrine of Our Lady of Knock, "the goal of my journey to Ireland", Pope John Paul II visited over two thousand sick people in the Church and concelebrated Mass in the open before over half a million. As at Guadalupe and Jasna Góra, the Pope appealed for trust and fidelity among Catholics, and for an enhanced devotion

to Mary "Mother of Christ and Mother of the Church".

It was the Pope's visit to Killineer near Drogheda, a town associated with religious conflict and bloodshed in Irish history, that riveted the attention of peoples and governments all over the world as they waited for him to pronounce on the persistence of violence in Ireland and its bitter internal divisions.

Those who heard the Pope in their hundreds of thousands seemed deeply moved. Some later complained that he was too evenhanded, or not specific enough in condemnation, but who knows what was or could still be the effect of his message on the bigots or the people of violence listening to him?

He talked naturally of Irish religious history: the coming of St

1 In front of the towering skyscrapers of New York.

2 A visit to the Living History Farm at Des Moines, which contains a museum of old farm implements as used by the first settlers.

Holy Mass at Des Moines.

Patrick and the foundation of the Primatial See of Armagh; and then of the martyrdom of St Oliver Plunkett.

This path led the Pope to the evil of violence. Even as a defender of the oppressed, he said, Oliver Plunkett would never have condoned violence. Nor was the present conflict taking place in Northern Ireland a religious war. "On the contrary, Catholics and Protestants, as people who confess Christ, taking inspiration from their faith and the Gospel, are seeking to draw closer to one another in unity and peace".

After quoting Pope Paul VI's words, that true peace must be founded on justice, Pope John Paul II, at the heart of his message, saying that peace could not be established by violence, emphatically joined his voice "to the voices of your religious leaders, to the voices of all men and women of reason, and I proclaim, with the conviction of my faith in Christ and with an awareness of my mission, that violence is evil, that violence is unacceptable as a solution to problems, that violence is unworthy of man".

To the men and women of violence, the Pope then appealed on his knees, in the name of God, to "return to Christ who died so that men might live in forgiveness and peace".

In moving and memorable

words, he extended this appeal to the young, to all those in positions of leadership, and to all those with political responsibility for the affairs of Ireland. They should respond to his presence in Drogheda on his "great mission of peace and reconciliation".

The Pope's hundreds of speeches made in so many different countries of the world express his own pre-occupations and cast of mind. Early drafts and help in composition and phrasing will naturally come more often than not from the Pope's advisers in the Curia. And the homilies and speeches the Pope makes abroad are often the fruits of his continuing dialogue with the bishops

of the world. When he visited the United States, for instance, he clearly based many of his discourses on what the American hierarchy on the whole thought would be salutary for their Catholic flock to hear.

When he flies round the world, the Pope has the custom of sending telegrams to the heads of states over which his aircraft soars. En route for Ireland, for instance, courteous little messages of esteem and prayer went to the President of Italy, the President of the Swiss Confederation, the President of the French Republic, to Queen Elizabeth and to the President of the Irish Republic.

From Ireland, the Pope flew directly to Boston in the United States. President Carter was in the White House, and the Pope's visit to him would mark a unique historical event. John Paul II seemed by his words in the United States chiefly to want to confirm the traditional faith and strengthen the unity of American Catholics under their bishops.

As always, he set a gruelling pace for those accompanying him: the bevy of journalists and photographers with whom he chatted amiably on the journey, members of his own Papal entourage, and his various hosts at odd stages of the visit.

After Boston, the Pope spoke on 2 October at the Yankee Stadium, New York, and on the same day to a group of Spanish-speaking immigrants in the Bronx. After morning prayer in St Patrick's Cathedral, on 3 October, he defied the rain to speak to 300,000 people in Battery Park, Manhattan. At Shea Stadium he was greeted in English, Polish and Italian, and replied in kind.

The same day, in Philadelphia, the Pope gave an address in the Cathedral and a homily that afternoon during a Mass at Kogan Circle. He talked to seminarians on the evening of 3 October, and on 4 October visited the tomb of St John Neumann before addres-

sing the Ukrainian community in their own cathedral. His last meeting in Philadelphia was with representatives of the councils of priests of all the dioceses of the United States, with whom he concelebrated Mass.

He visited farming communities in Des Moines on 4 October and went on to meet hundreds of the faithful in the Church of St Peter in Chicago. On 5 October he said Mass for the Polish Community in Chicago, and then delivered a homily to over a million people at Grant Park, by Lake Michigan.

On 5 October came the Pope's key meeting with the bishops of the United States at a seminary in Chicago, where the final tribute to him was a concert in his honour by the Chicago Symphony Orchestra, playing Bruckner's Fifth Symphony. On 6 October the Pope arrived in Washington where he met President Carter, with about 3000 invited guests, and delivered an appeal for disarmament before representatives at the Organisation of American States. He spoke also to people who had gathered outside the building, in Spanish as well as English.

In Washington on the evening of 6 October, the Pope addressed the diplomatic corps. On the second day of his sojourn in the United States, he had already delivered a forceful appeal for peace and human rights to the General Assembly of the United Nations. Thus, especially during his visit to the United States, John Paul II was able to throw into high relief the attention paid in the world of governments and diplomacy to the policies of the Holy See, and the Holy See's own anxiety to seize every opportunity to promote its message.

The Pope's long and carefully constructed address to the UN assembly contained a firm pledge of Papal support to the United Nations as "the forum of peace and justice". It expounded in detail the hopes of the Pope and his pre-

1   *The Pope addresses the General Assembly of the United Nations in New York.*

2   *John Paul II speaks to the crowds near the White House with the Capitol in the background.*

decessors for the achievement of world peace based on development and the readiness to sacrifice particular political interests. In an eloquent and lucid speech, the Pope again hammered home the theme of the dignity of the human person and the cause of religious freedom, asking (in the UN's Year of the Child) whether children were "to receive the arms race from us as a necessary inheritance".

So in his visit to the United States, John Paul II reviewed all the main themes of his Pontificate, looking outward from the Catholic Church to the world, and looking inward, especially when he spoke sternly to the American bishops, to warn that they must guard and teach "the sacred deposit of Christian Doctrine".

To American Catholics — the

50 million of them living in the very type of "consumer society" that the Pope often criticises for its materialism — the Pope had presented on his tour an image of great charm and strength of personality (whether joking in Harlem or singing in the Yankee Stadium). His reiteration of the Church's traditional teachings on such subjects as priestly celibacy, birth control, abortion, and general matters of ecclesiastical discipline, however, underlined the existence of dissension within the Catholic Church and the diamond-hard insistence of Pope John Paul II on a unified system of clearly stated belief.

2

The Vatican's busy round

The Pope returned to Rome from America on 8 October. His journeys of 1979 were rounded off when he flew to Turkey chiefly to foster the cause of Christian unity between East and West. His great sympathy for the Orthodox Churches appears to stem from his sensibilities as a Slav, born and nurtured in a country at the very centre of the whole of Europe, and from his istinctive, though reasoned, orthodoxy and traditionalism which are much in tune with the heritage of the Patriarchs.

The pattern and motivation of the Pope's travels through the world were clearly established in the great journeys of 1979. He stamped his personality on the post-Vatican II Catholic Church as a loving and inflexible teacher. His Polish nationality and sustained public defence of human rights and religious freedom magnified his importance as the spiritual leader of the world's Catholics in the struggle between the Communist countries and the West. The personal emphasis he brought to bear on the teachings of the Catholic Church and his genius as a communicator to people, made governments attend carefully to what he might say, concerning particular issues between states as well as general matters of war and peace, poverty and development.

The white-robed, thick-set figure standing in front of crowds of hundreds of thousands, and moving forward to meet them, unselfconsciously affectionate to all, and never seeming at a loss, was established as a world states-man of immense popularity and invulnerability.

In 1980, the Pope began to see more of Italy itself. He went to Umbria to celebrate the centenary of the birth of St Benedict, chosen patron saint of Europe and the founder of the monastic order of the Benedictines.

Reminders of the Pope's arduous life as head of the Holy See and the Curia and as ruler of the Vatican City State come from looking at some of his activities in the winter of 1979-80. A meeting of the Sacred College of Cardinals was called, in plenary assembly, partly to discuss the organisation of the government of the Church through the Curia; partly to look at the economic resources of the Holy See, which were being stretched and strained through its growing international commitments and through inflation. Later, the Pope would set up a committee of cardinals to look more carefully into the whole question of Vatican finances.

During those weeks, the Pope met and addressed the clergy of Rome, in the hall of the Lateran University. He gave the homily on a Sunday at one of the parishes of Rome, San Silvestro and San Martino. He visited the offices and studios of Vatican Radio at Palazzo Pio, near the Tiber, and talked to the broadcasters and technicians. He received in audience the Court of the Sacred Roman Rota, the tribunal dealing with marriage cases and problems within the Catholic Church.

In May 1980, John Paul II undertook a long and tiring journey outside Europe once more. He flew to Africa to visit Zaïre, Kenya, Ghana, Upper Volta and the Ivory Coast. There were colourful ceremonies and encounters, including the ordination of eight bishops at Kinshasa, an audience given to Muslim chiefs, and a visit to the leper colony at Adzope. On one unhappy day excitement over the Pope's presence led to many injuries and the death of several people through panic and pressure in the crowd.

Later that year the Pope visited France to deliver talks and addres-

48

1   Pope John Paul is welcomed to Africa by drums and dancing.

2   The Pope blesses a small child.

ses in Paris, the capital of the "eldest daughter of the Church" and to pray at the shrine of St Teresa of Lisieux. His first words to the French were to exhort them to be proud of their faith. Despite the weakening of the Catholic faith in France during the past decades, Pope John Paul received an especially generous and lively welcome from the young people he addressed. He welcomed the chance to speak to a session of the executive council of UNESCO on 2 June. Then, at the end of the month, he was on an aircraft to Brazil, impelled, as he said, "to confirm my fellow bishops in their mission".

In Brazil, there were indeed di-

sturbing political pressures caused by social unrest and harsh official policies. John Paul II travelled extensively throughout the country which staggers the eye and mind with its stupendous landscapes and potential wealth in both human and material terms. He plunged into Brazil's teeming life, from the frenetic industrial city of Sao Paolo to the fantastic capital of Brasilia, where he visited prisoners in gaol, the city slums and the Indian villages.

Brazil contains the largest Catholic population of any country in the world: a total of about 100 million. The Pope learnt Portuguese and so was able to let Brazilian leaders learn from his lips, in their own language, the sharp criticism the Holy See must make of bad social conditions and political victimisation. In one of the shanty towns of Rio, he twisted a gold ring from his finger and handed it to the local priest to be used to help the poor. To the workers of Sao Paolo he praised the dignity of work and its consonance with the creativity and nobility of man; a subject to be expanded in his most stimulating encyclical *Laborem Exercens* in September 1981.

Pope John Paul celebrates his last Mass in Manaus before leaving Brazil.

1 The Pope waves a greeting to the German Catholics who thronged to welcome him.

2 At an open-air Mass near Cologne Cathedral.

1

2

In the winter of 1980, Pope John Paul II toured the Federal Republic of Germany. He packed a heavy load of travel and talking into five days. Mostly, the topics dealt with ecumenism and married life. The Pope had expressed his definite and unshakeable views on certain problems of married life at the fifth Synod of Bishops held in Rome in September 1980. In Germany, as well as reiterating his teaching on birth control and abortion, the Pope offered hope and friendliness to those seeking the path leading to Christian unity.

The Pope's most ambitious and long-sighted foray into the world outside Europe took place early in 1981 when he left Rome for the Far East. First he went to Pakistan; then to meet the strongly Catholic peoples of the Philippines; then to talk to the Japanese with their very small Christian communities and their historically tragic cities with the names of Hiroshima and Nagasaki.

The Pope's journey to the Far East provided an opportunity for soundings to be taken in Hong Kong by the Cardinal Secretary of State, the Pope's right-hand man

3 The Pope gives his blessing to the faithful in the Philippines.

in diplomacy. For in its religious and diplomatic interests, the contacts and negotiations of the Holy See take it guardedly but hopefully into the Communist countries, including China.

From a different standpoint altogether, namely the relationships between the Roman Catholic and Anglican Churches, at the beginning of 1981 the prospect of a visit by John Paul II to Britain was beginning to require early planning. On 17 October 1980, on a very pleasant and magnificent occasion, the Pope had received Queen Elizabeth II and Prince Philip in the Apostolic Palace at the Vatican. The ceremonies were solemn and colourful in the best, though nowadays less elaborate, Vatican tradition, with a fanfare to greet the royal couple on their arrival by Rolls-Royce and an escort of Swiss Guards in dress uniforms to lead them towards the Papal apartments where they were met by his Holiness at the threshold of his library.

1   Pope John Paul speaks to the Japanese people at the city of Hiroshima where there was so much suffering at the end of World War II.

2   The Pope preaches at the Shrine of Our Lady at Fatima in Portugal.

2

The bid to kill the Pope

The hierarchies of England and Wales had separately invited the Pope to visit England, Wales and Scotland after he had given an audience to Cardinal Hume and Archbishop Worlock at his summer villa in 1980. The Pope's visit would be in 1982.

And then, on 13 May 1981, an attempt was made to assassinate Pope John Paul II in St Peter's Square.

On important occasions such as the election of a new Pope St Peter's Square will be crowded with nearly half a million people. This famous piazza in front of the great Basilica of St Peter's was designed by the sculptor and architect Bernini who defined its shape with the enciling arms of two colonnades. The huge semi-circular stone colonnades each have four rows of Doric columns, creating broad covered passages round the square. There were once plans for a third row of columns, "closing" the piazza. They were never built, and Bernini's colonnades are like open arms inviting the world to approach St Peter's and the palace of the Pope.

The gunman went to St Peter's Square not long before 5 o' clock in the afternoon. He asked where the Pope would appear and was given the wrong direction by a Benedictine monk. At 5 o' clock, the Pope appeared, being driven in a white jeep from the direction of the Gate of the Bells.

At 5.19 the gunman stood in front of the Pope's slowly moving vehicle which was heading towards the steps of the Basilica and fired two bullets from a distance of about nine feet. A nun tugged his jacket and spoilt his perfect aim. Otherwise, the Pope might have died instantly.

The name of the assassin was Mehemat Ali Agca. He had been

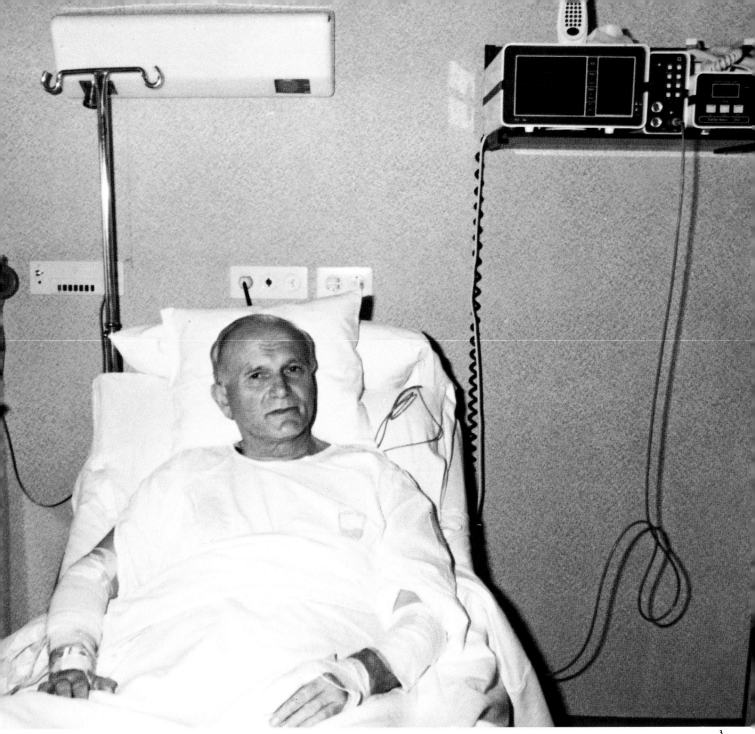

in prison in Turkey till he escaped in November 1979, and he had sworn to kill the Pope. He is now in an Italian gaol, condemned to life imprisonment. No evidence of conspiracy was brought forward at his trial but speculation about a plot against the Holy See inevitably continues. Agca may have been motivated only by Moslem extremism. Who knows?

His Holiness Pope John Paul II, who had been waving and smiling and reaching out to the people, collapsed and began to lose blood. He was taken quickly to the Gemelli hospital, a 20-minu-

1   Only a moment before the assassination attempt, Pope John Paul blesses the crowds of pilgrims in St Peter's Square.

2   The would-be assassin takes aim.

3   Pope John Paul recovers in Gemelli Hospital in Rome.

59

te drive. He had been wounded in the stomach, where one bullet penetrated the abdomen, and in the second finger of his right hand.

At the hospital, he had an immediate colostomy operation.

On Sunday 16 May he broadcast on Vatican Radio, saying as his first words, ''Jesus Christ be praised''. It seems that the Pope soon began to attribute his recovery, stage by stage, to the intercession of the Blessed Virgin Mary. Most of the world marvelled at his robust constitution and mental stamina. Although he suffered a relapse in early June and returned to hospital where he rested till 14 August, his health there-

after steadily improved and his energies, if not quite restored, appeared to be as vital as ever.

Almost a year to the day, on 12 May 1982, there was to be another attempted assault on the Pope during his visit to the Shrine of Our Lady at Fatima in Portugal. This time a Spanish priest approached him with a bayonet raised in his hand. The Pope seemed momentarily unaware of what was happening as the man, whom he turned to bless, was pulled to the ground.

At Fatima, the Pope showed yet once again, through the latest of his succession of modern-style pilgrimages to shrines and sanctuaries, the depth and simplicity

of his religious devotion to the Virgin Mary. In the diocese of Leiria in central Portugal, three shepherd children said, in May 1917, that they had seen the figure of a lady brighter than the sun, standing on a cloud in the foliage of a tree. She had asked them to return to the spot each month until October, when she would reveal what she wanted of them. By October, the crowd with the children had reached 50,000. The Lady disclosed herself to the children as Our Lady of the Rosary and many years later, the Church, through the local bishop, authorised the cult of Fatima, though not the many revelations and devotions since associated with it.

1 *The Pope blesses the other patients from his hospital window.*

2 *Pope John Paul in his private chapel in the Vatican.*

Back to Africa

Well before the second attempt on the Pope's life his health and vigour were sufficiently recovered for him to pay a second "apostolic visit" to Africa. From 12-19 February 1982 he visited Nigeria, Benin, Gabon and Equatorial Guinea. Shortly before he began the flight from Rome (pausing to visit the new Fiumicino chapel dedicated to Our Lady of Loreto) he had given his annual address when receiving the diplomatic corps in Rome. Recently, too, he had welcomed to the Vatican the bishops of Nigeria on their special visit and also the new Nigerian Ambassador to the Holy See.

The Pope was able to announce to the diplomats assembled in the Consistorial Hall of the Vatican on 16 January that from the same day the Legation of Great Britain to the Holy See had been raised to the rank of embassy, while an Apostolic Nunciature in place of a delegation had been instituted in London, with a Pro-Nuncio as Head of Mission.

His reasons for going to Nigeria, the Pope told the new Nigerian Ambassador were "pastoral": he would meet many of his brothers and sisters in Christ, greet the members of other religions, especially those of the Muslim faith, and talk to the leaders of the nation during his journey of "friendship and faith".

When he left Lagos for Benin on 17 February, sending a message "of brotherhood, friendship and love" to every Nigerian child, John Paul II delivered a farewell address glowing with praise

for his host country. "I take away with me very vivid memories of a great nation, a generous people, a dynamic Church, a richly endowed and warm-hearted youth, a country which honours the family, respects the elderly and regards children as a blessing...".

Then, in the early months of 1982, the Pope's series of apostolic journeys began to be affected by the eruption of the very violence within nations and between nations against which his preaching to the world was so vehemently directed.

During the time he was visiting the shrine at Fatima in Portugal,

and being greeted as the "Pope of the workers" in Oporto, the outbreaks of civil conflict continued in his beloved Poland, and the dispute between the United Kingdom and Argentina over the Falkland Islands grew more intense and warlike.

Pope John Paul II sent a message in advance of his visit to Britain, asking for God's blessing on the country to enable her "to fulfill her exalted destiny in justice and in peace". In a brave act of conciliation the Pope asked cardinals from Britain and Argentina to come to the Vatican to say Mass and to pray for peace together.

1 *In 1982 the Pope returned to Africa to visit Nigeria, Benin, Gabon and Equatorial Guinea.*

2 *As always the children attracted Pope John Paul's immediate attention.*

An apostle in Britain

Throughout history, relations between the Papacy and the United Kingdom have been enormously intense, veering from bitter dispute even before the Protestant Reformation, to great loyalty and devotion in medieval times, and growing respect in the recent past.

Pope Gregory the Great, who saw some young English slaves in Rome and said they were not English but angels — *non Angli sed Angeli* — sent Augustine with 30 other monks to preach to the English nation in AD 597, and St Augustine established his episcopal See of Canterbury.

A Christian country ever since, England has been profoundly influenced in her history and culture by the Catholic Church, despite the Reformation, and after a

gap of centuries, the English Roman Catholic hierarchy was restored by Pope Pius IX in 1850.

For his visit to Britain, Pope John Paul II chose as his theme the seven sacraments. These are a distinctive hallmark of the theology of the Catholic Church, being sometimes defined as the outward signs of invisible grace which were ordained by Christ Himself and which, centred among themselves on the Eucharist, constitute acts of faith, celebrations of the Church and the means to salvation.

Catholics believe in the validity of the seven sacraments of the New Law namely, the Eucharist, Baptism, Confirmation, Penance, Marriage, Holy Orders, and Annointing of the Sick.

As well as preaching and admi-

1   On 28 May the Pope arrived at Gatwick Airport on the first day of his historic visit to England. He was greeted by the Duke and Duchess of Norfolk and by Cardinal Hume (left) and Cardinal Gray, the Roman Catholic primates of England and Scotland.

2-3-4   On the first day of his visit the Pope conducted a Mass in Westminster Cathedral in London, which was attended by all the Bishops of England and Wales.

2

3

4

nistering the sacraments, Pope John Paul II came to Britain to remind his own flock of the age-old veneration in the country of the Virgin Mary, exemplified especially at the shrine of Walsingham.

The invitation to the Pope came separately from the hierarchies of England and Wales, and Scotland respectively, and both made their own arrangements for the reception of the most travelled and familiar Pope in history.

The historic visit to Britain began on Friday 28 May, when the aircraft bringing the Pope from Rome landed at Gatwick, in the Surrey countryside south of London. Immediately the Pope went to Westminster Cathedral, near the Thames in the heart of London, where he celebrated Mass with all the bishops of England and Wales. Then he was driven in bright sunshine through the centre of London to Buckingham Palace for a quiet talk with the Queen. In the afternoon, the Pope visited another of London's famous Catholic cathedrals, St George's in Chaucer's Southwark, just south of the Thames, where he held a

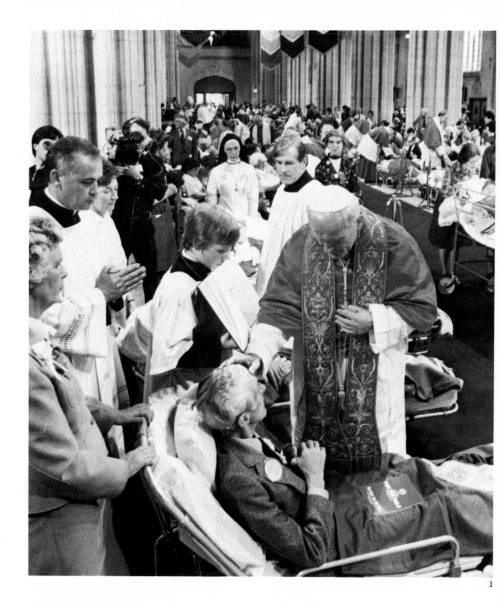

1   On 28 May Pope John Paul visited St George's Cathedral in Southwark, London, where he gave his blessing to the sick and disabled and also administered last rites to people who were terminally ill.

2   As a gesture of friendship and esteem, Dr Runcie presented to the Pope a portrait of the great martyr St Thomas Becket.

service for the old people and the sick, the mentally handicapped and those fatally ill.

An event to which many Britons had looked forward with faith, hope and charity was the Pope's visit to Canterbury Cathedral to take part in a service, at the invitation of the Archbishop of Canterbury, Dr Robert Runcie. As well as worshipping in the entrancing Gothic cathedral with his Anglican brethren, the Pope held private discussions in Canterbury with other church leaders. No dramatic communiqués were expected or produced, but for many these talks were the main substance of the Papal visit to Britain, confirming the slow but sure movement of the Christian Churches towards greater unity.

For most ordinary people, the great event of the Pope's first few days in England was the Mass which he celebrated before thousands of worshippers at Wembley Stadium.

On Whit Sunday (his memory surely returning to the Pentecost he spent in Poland the year after he became Pope) John Paul II met the people of Coventry and said

3 In Canterbury, at the home of Dr Runcie, the Pope was greeted by Prince Charles who also attended the service in the Cathedral.

4 On 29 May the Pope visited Canterbury where he attended a service in Canterbury Cathedral together with Archbishop Runcie. It was a moving and important meeting of the two Christian Churches.

Pope landed at the RAF airfield at Turnhouse near Edinburgh on 31 May, Whit Monday, and in the evening met tens of thousands of young Scots at the Murrayfield Stadium. He went by motorcade to meet the Moderator General and give an address at Edinburgh Cathedral. His last hours in Scotland were devoted to talks with Church leaders, a visit to the sick in hospital, talks with nuns and priests, and, after he had said Mass in Bellahouston Park, a quiet supper with the Scottish bishops.

In Wales, where the numbers of Roman Catholics has grown appreciably in recent years, the Pope found himself talking Polish to many of his compatriots who have found freedom in Britain and whom he had earlier met in their thousands at Crystal Palace in the south of England. It was a day of meeting and animated conversation in and around Cardiff, and in Ninian Park with civic leaders, thousands of young people, and the Welsh clergy. But the most moving and dramatic event was the Mass which the Pope said in Pontcanna Fields where he drove around in an atmosphere of tremendous fervour. A cavalcade accompanied John Paul II through the countryside from Culver Cross to Cardiff Airport and his jet aircraft for Rome. World peace and reconciliation between nations; social justice within nations; unity and love between the Christian Churches: these were the strong themes of the Pope's historic journey through England, Scotland and Wales.

When John Paul II was elected Pope in the Autumn of 1978, the *Times* newspaper, in its first editorial leader, commented that the event was one of extreme importance. This was not just because he was non-Italian and comparatively young for a Pope. It was because as a Pole ''he has a very particular experience of some of the greatest problems that confront the Church...''

1-2 From Canterbury the Pope flew by helicopter to Wembley Stadium where enormous crowds had gathered in the sunshine to welcome him and to attend Mass.

3 On 30 May Pope John Paul was greeted by thousands of Polish immigrants at Crystal Palace. Just as he spoke in English, Welsh and Scottish Gaelic on other occasions during his trip, here he made his address in his own native language of Polish.

Mass there. In the afternoon he talked to enthusiastic crowds at Speke Airport and continued the ecumenical emphasis of his journey by visiting the Anglican Cathedral before saying Mass at the Metropolitan Cathedral of Liverpool.

John Paul II's delight in addressing huge crowds and welcoming people, in getting near to and acknowledging the individuals among them so that the crowds are seen as truly human, was in evidence most of all at the open-air Mass which he said at Heaton Park, Manchester, and before the large gathering of people on the Knavesmire, York.

Welcomed by bagpipes, the

1   *From London on Whit Sunday Pope John Paul flew to Coventry to hold an open-air Mass at the airport.*

2-3-4   *The last journey of Whit Sunday was made by helicopter to Liverpool where the Pope was welcomed to the Anglican*

Cathedral by David Shepherd, Bishop of Liverpool.

2

3

4

1   Pope John Paul then made his way by motorcade to the Roman Catholic Metropolitan Cathedral of Liverpool where he conducted a Mass.

2-3   On 31 May, at Heaton Park in Manchester, the Pope attended the ordination of several priests and conducted an open-air Mass.

4   Enthusiastic crowds welcomed Pope John Paul to the Knavesmire racecourse at York on Whit Monday, 31 May.

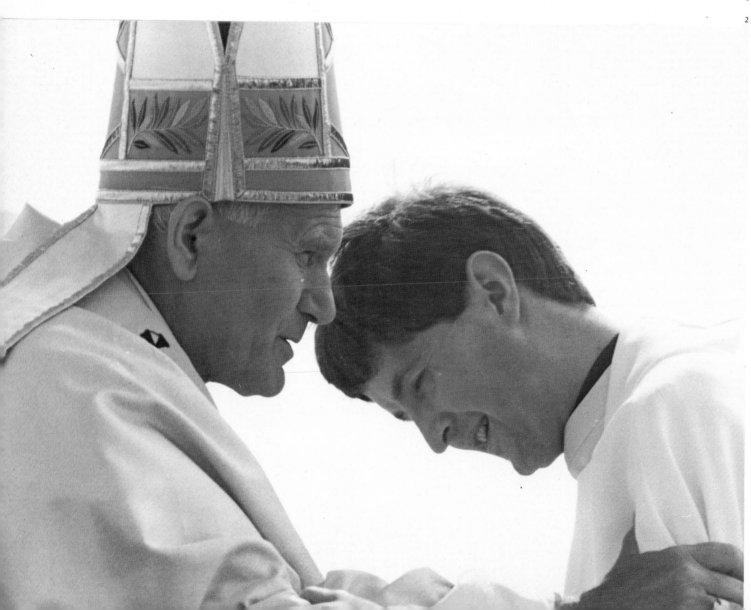

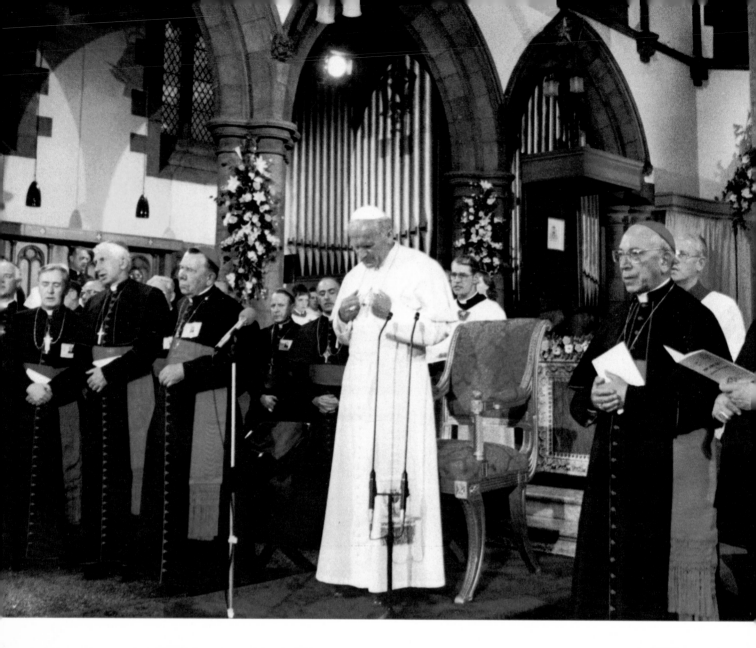

Since then, the nationalism in Pope John Paul's heart and mind has if anything been strengthened. He remains a very Polish Pope. But through his extraordinary journeys throughout the world he has increasingly grown into an international Pope by understanding, as well as by fame.

The understanding he has gained as Supreme Pastor is primarily that of the problems and worries of the Roman Catholic bishops and clergy and the Catholic faithful in the different continents and countries of the world.

The Pope's reaction to experiencing these at first hand, and to his own nearness to death, has been to strengthen his own faith in the traditional teachings of the Catholic Church and his determination to teach them.

1   From York the Pope flew to Edinburgh where he was welcomed to Edinburgh Cathedral.

2-3   From Edinburgh Pope John Paul flew to Glasgow where a Mass was held on 1 June at Bellahouston Park. Following the Mass the Pope planted a small oak tree to commemorate his visit.

75

1   This, for many, is the hard side of the Pope; for many others, it is the facet of his character that brings most reassurance. For nearly all, however, the warmth and kindliness of his personality and his courage have brought an uplifting of the spirit and a renewal of faith in what the Pope himself so firmly emphasises: the dignity and potential of the human being.

The importance of the Pope's visit to Britain was primarily for Catholics in England, Wales and Scotland: for them to see and hear the teaching of the successor of St Peter. For the community as a whole, it brought into their midst, in search of some better understanding, a man who is among the world's greatest and most influential living statesmen. For members of the other Churches, the presence of the Pope was reassuring as much where it indicated the long way still to go to Christian unity, as where it showed that the desire for unity is sincerely there, in the Holy See.

1   *On 2 June, the last day of his visit to Great Britain, Pope John Paul flew to Cardiff where he was greeted by the Archbishop of Cardiff, Monsignor John Murphy. As is his custom on arriving in a new country, the Pope knelt to kiss the ground.*

2   *In Cardiff the Pope received the Freedom of the City.*

3   *An open-air Mass was held at Pontcanna Fields, attended by hundreds of thousands who had waited eagerly for this memorable day.*

Pope John Paul's last public engagement in Wales was at a gathering of young people in Ninian Park, Cardiff. Here he spoke of the importance of world peace and his words were greeted with great applause.

ACKNOWLEDGEMENTS

Writing this book would have been difficult without the characteristic helpfulness and patience of my wife. It would have been impossible without the files of *The Universe*, *The Tablet*, and *L'Osservatore Romano*.

Many details concerning the Pope's life have been gleaned from the pages of several books from diverse pens over the last few months. They all testify to the amazing effect of Pope John Paul II. My select list is:

John Paul II A Man from Krakow George Blazynski, London 1979;

Man from a Far Country Mary Craig, London (paperback revised edition) 1982;

Pope John Paul II An authorised biography Lord Longford, London 1982;

Pope John Paul II and the Catholic Restoration Paul Johnson, London 1982;

Introducing John Paul II Peter Hebblethwaite, London (paperback) 1982;

Pope John Paul II His Travels and Missions Norman St John Stevas, London 1982.

And my own book *Inside the Vatican*, London 1982.